Copyright Page

So Here We Are

A Darkly Humorous Guide to Surviving the Unthinkable

This book is a work of satire and survival commentary. It is intended for informational and entertainment purposes only. The author and publisher assume no responsibility for the use or misuse of the information contained herein.

ISBN: 979-8-9988889-2-2

Publisher: **Independent Release**
Printed in the United States of America
First Edition

Built with duct tape, sarcasm, and open-source tools: **GIMP, LibreOffice, and a barely-functioning AI.**

So Here We Are
A Restored Cold War Survival Guide for the World We Hoped We'd Never See

Table of Contents

Section IV – Appendices & Extras

"Because information still matters"

INEXPLICABLY
LEFT BLANK

(For all my government document readers)

Section 1

You're Still Alive — For Now

A Practical Guide to the First 24 Hours of Not Dying

Lesson 1.

Yeah..So That Just Happened

Congratulations! You've just survived a nuclear detonation. Either by blind luck, thick walls, divine intervention, or the simple fact that you weren't important enough to be near Ground Zero. Whatever the reason — you're still here.

Your reward? A front-row seat to one of humanity's most preventable achievements.

Let's not sugarcoat it: the power just died, your phone's out, there's glass in your shoe, and you may or may not be glowing slightly. The bad news? This is the *easy* part, it just gets harder from here. The good news? You have this guide.

We'll navigate you through the critical next 24 hours with just enough humor to keep your panic attacks playful.

Lesson 2.

You Best Check Yourself

Before you pretend to be useful to anyone else, run a quick diagnostic on your meat suit.

Look for:

- Burns (first, second, or "crispy")

- Bleeding (you'll know it when you see it)

- Disorientation (if you think it's 1997, sit down)

- Coughing blood or vomit (bad)

- Extra fingers (congrats, you're evolving)

If you've got a working flashlight, use it. If you've got a mirror, check your eyes — blown pupils may signal a concussion, or that you're just really freaked out. Either way, don't operate heavy machinery.

Lesson 3.

The 7–10 Rule, or: Why You Shouldn't Lick the Dirt Yet

Here's nuclear physics, distilled into something even a fallout roach could understand:

> For every **7 times** the amount of time since the blast, radiation levels drop by **a factor of 10**.

In simple terms:

- After 1 hour, radiation is still 🔥

- After 7 hours, it's 1/10th as bad

- After 49 hours, it's 1/100th

- After 2 weeks, you might be able to sunbathe again (don't)

What this means:
Stay under as much dense stuff as possible — dirt, concrete, books about economics — for the first **48–72 hours**. Every hour you're not pretending to be Mad Max is an hour you're not irradiating your insides.

Lesson 4.

Take Cover, Not Comfort

You need a shelter. No, not your vinyl-sided house with the bay windows. You need **mass between you and the sky**.

Best options (ranked by survival, not style):

1. Basement under concrete building

2. Subway station or underground garage

3. Interior bathroom, surrounded by furniture and earth-filled bags

4. Hole in the ground + tarp + 18 inches of dirt

5. Not your car. Not even your cousin's Hummer.

Block windows. Seal vents. Stay put. Do not open doors to investigate "weird glows." That's how B-movies start.

Lesson 5.

Water: The Other Fallout

You will need water long before you need answers. Fallout particles can contaminate open water sources — but not all is lost.

DO:

- Drink from sealed containers (bottled water, cans, toilet tank*)
- Use water from hot water heaters or radiator tanks (if intact)
- Purify with:
    - Bleach (2 drops/qt, wait 30 min)
    - Boiling (10+ mins)

"Yes, the toilet tank — the part that fills with water. Not the bowl, you savage."

DO NOT:

- Drink rainwater within the first week
- Drink from puddles, open lakes, or things labeled "mystical spring"

Lesson 6.

You've Got 24 Hours to Not Screw This Up

Print this on your mental clipboard:

- ✅ Get underground or under mass
- ✅ Stay inside for at least 72 hours
- ✅ Collect safe water and seal it
- ✅ Do not cook outside or start fires

☑ Monitor symptoms: nausea, confusion, bleeding gums = bad
☑ If you have potassium iodide, take it NOW (before exposure)

Optional:
☑ Write "Alive" in large letters on your roof with tar or paint
☑ Start naming cockroaches for company

Closing Note

You're still alive — for now. If you can make it through the next few days, you'll likely live long enough to:

- Curse your old HOA for banning fallout shelters

- Barter for beans with a man named Sludge

- Read the rest of this guide

Let's keep going. The world didn't end. It just got weirder.

Section II
Declassified Civil Defense Protocols

Lesson 7.

Fallout Shelter Construction Basics

Adapted from U.S. Civil Defense Guidance (1967–1975)

"Your House Won't Save You. But Your Basement Might."

The Cold War U.S. government believed in two things:

1. That nuclear war was survivable.

2. That average Americans could build something that wouldn't collapse under its own optimism.

This chapter restores real shelter designs distributed to the public between 1960 and 1975 — edited for clarity, practicality, and our shared reality. They are built on a simple principle:

Mass = Survival.
The more dense stuff between you and fallout, the better.

No lasers. No bunkers with espresso machines. Just bricks, dirt, plywood, and optimism.

Shelter Type 1: The Basement Lean-To

"The "please-don't-crush-me" triangle."

How it works:
Construct a low A-frame wedge against a sturdy basement wall, then bury it under heavy material — earth, water jugs, books, or whatever you've hoarded.

Materials Needed:

- 6 sheets of 3/4" plywood

- 20 cinder blocks (or 300+ books)

- Plastic sheeting (for waterproofing)

- Blankets, insulation, or coats for warmth

- Duct tape. Always duct tape.

Protection Factor (PF): ~40

> PF 40 = You're receiving 1/40th the radiation dose compared to outside.
> That's the difference between "hospital stay" and "open-casket speedrun."

Setup Tips:

- Stack shielding over and around the lean-to (not just on top).

- Elevate sleeping surface slightly to avoid basement seepage.

- Don't block your own airflow. You need to breathe. Mostly.

Shelter Type 2: Above-Ground Core Shelter

"The Denial Box"

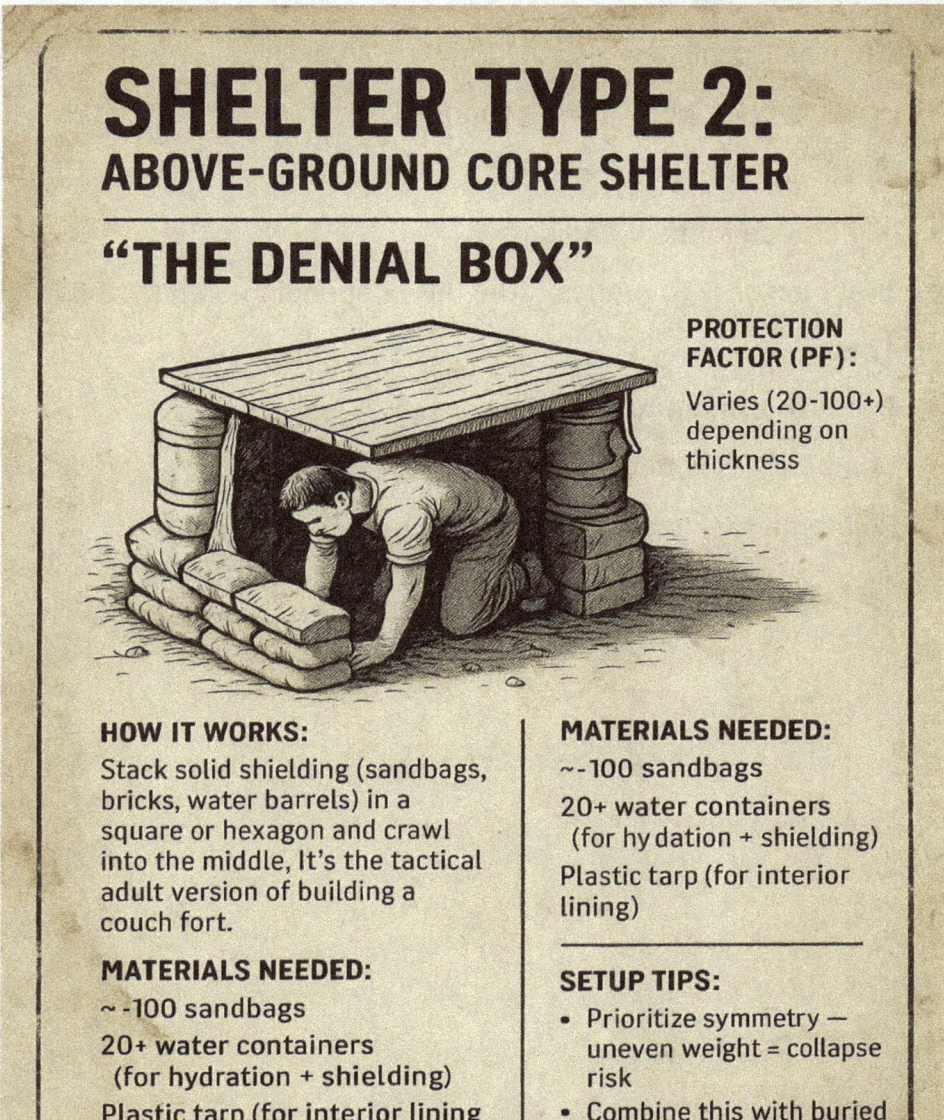

SHELTER TYPE 2:
ABOVE-GROUND CORE SHELTER

"THE DENIAL BOX"

PROTECTION FACTOR (PF):

Varies (20-100+) depending on thickness

HOW IT WORKS:
Stack solid shielding (sandbags, bricks, water barrels) in a square or hexagon and crawl into the middle, It's the tactical adult version of building a couch fort.

MATERIALS NEEDED:
~-100 sandbags
20+ water containers (for hydration + shielding)
Plastic tarp (for interior lining

MATERIALS NEEDED:
~-100 sandbags
20+ water containers (for hydation + shielding)
Plastic tarp (for interior lining)

SETUP TIPS:
- Prioritize symmetry — uneven weight = collapse risk
- Combine this with buried positioning if possible

How it works:
Stack solid shielding (sandbags, bricks, water barrels) in a square or hexagon and crawl into the middle. It's the tactical adult version of building a couch fort.

Materials Needed:

- ~100 sandbags

- 20+ water containers (for hydration + shielding)

- Scrap lumber for roof and supports

- Plastic tarp (for interior lining)

- A tolerance for very bad smells

Protection Factor (PF): Varies (20–100+) depending on thickness

Setup Tips:

- Prioritize symmetry — uneven weight = collapse risk

- Combine this with buried positioning if possible

- Reinforce roof to avoid "death by gravity"

Shelter Type 3: Trench Shelter (Improvised Earth Pit)

"Going full Hobbit, under duress"

How it works:
Dig a trench (3–4 feet deep), lay boards across the top, and cover with 18+ inches of earth. Waterproof the interior and seal both ends with makeshift doors.

Materials Needed:

- Shovel, and a will to live

- Scrap lumber or metal sheeting

- Plastic tarp or trash bags

- Dirt. Lots of it.

Protection Factor (PF): 100+

> Earth is one of the most effective shielding materials per inch. The downside? You're now an earthworm with a heartbeat.

Setup Tips:

- Dig on high ground to avoid flooding

- Create air vent at one or both ends

- Mark entrance with something non-flammable and obvious

General Shelter-Building Notes

- **Mass > Distance**
  More mass is better than more space. Tight quarters are survivable. A fallout migraine is not.

- **No Fire, No Fumes**
  Don't cook inside unless you like hallucinating and dying simultaneously.

- **Water = Protection + Life**
  Store water around the shelter to absorb radiation. It's dual-use shielding.

- **Airflow**
  Seal the shelter, *but not hermetically*. You need passive or manual airflow.

- **Test Crawl**
  If you can't get in and out in the dark while panicked — it's not good enough.

Final Checklist: "Can This Shelter Save Me?"

- ✅ 18 inches of solid mass on all sides (earth, water, books, concrete)
- ✅ Structural integrity (doesn't collapse if you breathe wrong)

☑ Access to air and water
☑ Space for at least 1 person to lie flat
☑ No glass, flammable materials, or overhead hazards
☑ You can stay in it for 72 hours without losing your mind (too much)

Sidebar: "Why Books Save Lives (Finally)"

The U.S. Office of Civil Defense once suggested stacking books around your shelter walls. Not for morale — for shielding.

A stack of 20–30 tightly packed hardcovers is dense enough to reduce radiation exposure by over 50%.

"Congratulations, your neglected library might finally justify its shelf space. Plus now you have a nuclear survival guide, radiation shielding and toilet paper all in one book."

Lesson 8.

Shelter Management: Duties, Morale, and Discipline

Adapted from U.S. Office of Civil Defense & FEMA internal guides (1965–1978)

> *"You may have built the shelter to survive the bomb. Now you have to survive each other."*

Civil defense officials quickly realized that **a well-stocked shelter still fails without leadership, order, and boundaries**. Whether you're stuck with your family, your neighbors, or a few strangers with strong opinions about canned beans — chaos kills faster than radiation.

This chapter restores Cold War-era shelter protocols for internal management, updated with a few hard-earned lessons from the 21st century:

- People panic
- People hoard
- People smell
- People make terrible decisions. And it's worse under pressure

Your job, or someone's, is to **run the shelter like your life depends on it.** Because it does.

The Role of the Shelter Manager (Yes, That Might Be You)

Every shelter needs a designated **manager**, regardless of size. This isn't about ego. It's about triage, rationing, and structure.

Primary duties include:

- Enforcing quiet hours and behavior norms
- Keeping a schedule (light, sleep, meals, latrine)
- Managing food/water inventory

- Preventing fights, breakdowns, or impulsive exits

- Monitoring health and symptoms

- Coordinating with any outside communications (if available)

Structure = Survival

Without time, there is madness. The old manuals were clear: **you must simulate normalcy** even when the world is ash.

Sample Shelter Schedule:

Time	Activity
0700	Wake / light routine
0730	Morning water ration + sanitation
0830	Quiet time / meditation / reading
1000	Ventilation / shelter check
1200	Main meal
1300	Conversation, morale check, games
1500	Rest period
1800	Evening water ration
1900	Light shutoff / prep for sleep
2000–0700	Silent hours

Why? Because people unravel without rhythm.
Why silent hours? Because radiation isn't the only thing that builds up in the dark.

Rationing Discipline: Fairness vs. Feelings

Water and food are finite. Fair distribution isn't optional — it's the only way the group survives intact.

> *"Just this once" becomes a riot by Day 2."*

Enforce:

- **Equal portions** unless medically required

- **Visible rationing** (no private stashes)

- **Inventory logs** updated daily

- **Zero tolerance for theft or hoarding**

Shelter guides advised creating a **ledger system**, even on paper scraps. What matters is that everyone sees the rules being followed.

Behavioral Problems (and How to Defuse Them)

The guides expected panic. So should you. Here's how to manage it:

Behavior	Suggested Response
Crying/panic	Comfort, don't shame. Assign small tasks.
Silence/apathy	Check for dehydration or shock.
Anger/disruption	Remove from group area, speak calmly.
Hoarding/stealing	Publicly address, reassert rationing rules.
Attempt to leave shelter	Block calmly, explain risk. Assign "Lookout Duty" near exit.

Note: If someone becomes violent and threatens others,
*you **must** isolate them if possible. Survival trumps diplomacy.*

Hygiene & Morale

"Clean people are calmer people." – *Civil Defense   Handbook, 1973*

Key Hygiene Rules:

- Assign latrine duty on a rotating basis (yes, rotate)
- Clean hands before ration time
- Ventilate the shelter for 15–30 mins every 12 hours
- Use bleach, vinegar, or alcohol to wipe surfaces if available

Morale Tools (Besides False Hope):

- Rotate books, jokes, or even songs

- Assign roles to everyone: "cook," "cleaner," "lookout," etc.

- Create a basic radio log or "outside report" if using emergency frequencies

- Record one positive or neutral observation per person daily

"Your beard makes you look 15% more radiation-proof."

Final Guidance: You Don't Need to Be a Leader — Just a Dam

A good shelter manager isn't charismatic. They're **a sandbag with a clipboard** — someone who stops chaos from leaking in until help arrives, or the world outside decays enough to poke your head out.

Set rules. Keep them.
A well-run shelter doesn't feel like prison.
A badly-run shelter becomes one.

Checklist: Shelter Manager's Daily Duties

- Confirm headcount and wellness
- Check food and water logs
- Monitor for illness/injury
- Rotate airflow system
- Assign cleaning and sanitation tasks
- Reiterate rationing policy
- Check for emotional instability
- Maintain quiet hours

Lesson9.

Radiological Monitoring & Dosimetry

How to Measure Death in Micrograms per Hour

> *"The good news: radiation is invisible.*
> *The bad news: radiation is invisible."*

You can't see it, smell it, or taste it — but it's there, whispering sweet mutations to your internal organs. This chapter teaches you how to detect, interpret, and survive radioactive fallout using Cold War-era tools, DIY approximations, and a little math.

Let's learn how to tell if that metallic dust on your windowsill is just ash — or the thing that's going to melt your chromosomes.

The Three Radiation Killers

The U.S. Office of Civil Defense (and basic physics) taught us that radiation sickness isn't just about "being near the bomb." There are three types of radiation concern post-detonation:

1. **Initial Radiation** (from the blast itself): If you're alive, you missed this one.

2. **Residual Radiation** (aka Fallout): Fine radioactive dust falling from the sky.

3. **Induced Radiation**: Normal stuff made radioactive by neutron exposure. (Fun.)

    For the next 2 weeks, **fallout is your main concern.**

The 7/10 Rule Revisited

As introduced earlier:

> For every 7× increase in time after detonation, radiation drops by 10×.

Here's a simplified table:

Time Since Blast	% of Original Radiation	Comment
1 hour	100%	🔥 Death soup
7 hours	~10%	Still not fun
2 days (49 hrs)	~1%	Survivable with shelter
2 weeks	~0.1%	Begin considering "outside"

This decay curve is **why sheltering for 72+ hours matters** more than anything else.

Fallout Detection: Cold War Tools

1. Geiger-Müller Counters

- Measures counts per minute (CPM) or mR/hr (milliroentgens/hour)
- Requires batteries, calibration, and luck
- Common Cold War models: CD V-700 (low-range), CD V-715 (high-range)

How to Use:

- Test air, food, and surfaces
- Hold probe near suspected fallout zones
- Listen for click rate — faster = bad

Warning:
Most vintage detectors **can't measure high doses accurately** — they overload.
CD V-715 only kicks in *after* it's already very dangerous.

2. Kearny Fallout Meter (KFM)

> *"When you need a dosimeter but only have soup cans and string."*

The KFM was a **DIY fallout meter** developed by Oak Ridge National Laboratory, designed to be built by anyone using household items and a printed scale. (some assembly and more detailed instructions required)

Requires:

- Aluminum foil

- Plastic jar or soup can

- Charged electroscope

- A steady hand and a belief in analog physics

Accuracy: ±25%
Modern Translation: Impressively effective. Also: deeply inconvenient.

DIY Radiation Monitoring (Low-Tech Methods)

If you have **none** of the above, here's how to get "good enough" data:

1. Dust Watch

- Place white sheets of paper or ceramic tiles outside shelter

- Check for greyish fallout over time (1–6 hours post-blast)

- Collect samples using gloves + mask

- If available, measure with Geiger counter at 1 foot distance

2. "Sick Clock" Method

- Monitor shelter occupants for:

    - Nausea/vomiting (starts ~2–6 hours after 100+ R exposure)

    - Fatigue, headache, skin burns

- Use timing to estimate dose exposure
  (e.g., Vomiting within 2 hours = 300+ R = not great.)

Interpreting Readings (mR/hr or R/hr)

Exposure (R)	Symptoms	Outcome
50 R	None	Safe, low dose
100 R	Mild nausea	Recoverable
200–400 R	Vomiting, hair loss	Recovery possible
600+ R	Severe illness	50% fatal without medical aid
1000+ R	CNS damage	Likely fatal within days

Rule of Thumb:

> If levels are over **100 mR/hr**, stay put.
> If your counter maxes out and screams, *definitely* stay put.

Final Notes: Track, Don't Panic

Radiation is scary because it's invisible. But it's predictable.

- Shelter time is your greatest weapon
- Old-school tools still work
- DIY solutions are better than ignorance
- Never assume the air is "probably fine"

Quick Radiation Assessment Kit

Tool	Source	Use
Geiger Counter	eBay, surplus, HAM communities	Direct measurement
KFM Printout	nukepills.com	Build-your-own
White ceramic tile	Kitchen/bath	Fallout spotting
Potassium Iodide	Medical prep supply	Thyroid protection (see Appendix)

> *"When in doubt, wait it out. The dirt outside will outlive the fire inside."*

Lesson 10.

Food Storage, Cooking, and Sanitation

> *"Because glowing in the dark is bad, but diarrhea in a sealed shelter is worse."*

You've made it through the blast, the panic, and the questionable decision to barricade yourself in a root cellar with six cans of beans and a cousin you barely like. Congratulations. Now it's time to talk about humanity's least glamorous biological needs: **eating and excreting without dying or becoming a health hazard**.

Let's take a dignified tour through your gastrointestinal future.

> *"The bomb didn't kill you. But bad chili in a sealed shelter might."*

Food Storage: Or, "Beans Again? Delightful."

Golden Rules:

- Shelf-stable wins over gourmet.

- Calories matter more than complaints.

- Variety is a lie we tell ourselves to keep hope alive.

"If it doesn't scream 'I was abandoned in a FEMA   warehouse in 1993' when you open it, it's probably not built for this scenario."

Minimum Daily Ration Per Adult:

- **Calories**: 1,200–2,000. Depends on how much effort you're putting into panic.

- **Water**: 1 gallon/day. No, coffee doesn't count. Nice try though.

The Big Three Food Groups:

1. **Canned Everything**: If it clangs, it lasts.

2. **Dry Goods**: Rice, oats, instant mash — aka "flavorless survival snow."

3. **Morale Boosters**: Chocolate, hot sauce, or a single mystery Twinkie to be worshipped as divine.

Pro tip: Canned peaches are now currency. Guard them with your life.

Avoid These "Rookie Rations":

- Bread (unless it doubles as insulation)

- Yogurt (yes, someone always tries)

- Any cheese that isn't classified as a spackle substitute

- "Organic trail mix" — this is no time for optimism

Cooking in a Sealed Tomb

> *"The menu tonight: slight warmth with a side of carbon monoxide risk."*

Your options are limited. You're not hosting a dinner party — you're warming glop in a hole.

🔥 Approved Heat Sources	Notes
Sterno	Burns slow, smells like "not dying yet"
Alcohol stoves	As safe as a 50-year-old blueprint can promise
Esbit tablets	Smells like regret, burns clean
No-cook rations	The real MVP: open, grimace, eat cold

Warning Signs:

- Smoke: Bad

- Fire: Worse

- "Smells like burning plastic" — evacuate, even if that means spooning dirt

Sanitation: The True Fallout

"Shelter Rule #1: Don't become the biohazard you're hiding from."

Bathroom time in a fallout shelter is where modesty dies.

The Bucket:

- 5 gallons. No shame.

- Line it. Double-bag it. Apologize to the next user.

- Layer in sawdust, kitty litter, or shredded tax documents.

  "Give it a name. Talk to it. It will know you better than anyone else after 72 hours."

"Advanced" Waste Strategy:

- Separate solids and liquids (if you care about odor…or self-respect)

- Build a lid (air-tight > dignity)

- Store full bags outside the living area. **Far** outside. Possibly downwind of your memories.

Hygiene Like Civilization Depends on It

Item	Usage
Hand sanitizer	Baptize your hands hourly
Bleach (5%)	For wiping surfaces and maybe your soul
Baby wipes	For pits, bits, and everything in between
Paper towels	If you have them, you're shelter royalty
Deodorant	Optional. Regret from your bunkmates is not.

Contamination Control: The "Don't Die From a Door Handle" Protocol

- Anything from outside is guilty until disinfected
- Bleach, soap water, or fire (kidding… mostly)
- Strip outer packaging
- Create a "filthy zone" just inside shelter entrance
- Anyone who sneezes near the food loses food privileges for the day

Shelter Cuisine Psychology

Long-term survival is a mental game. You'll need more than calories — you'll need **hope, ritual, and a pinch of denial**.

Tips:

- Assign a "Chef" (who just rotates cans and pretends to choose)
- Name your meals: "Tuesday Tuna Stack" sounds better than "Can #3"
- Celebrate the end of each day with a single square of chocolate and the crushing realization you still can't go outside

Quick Checklist: Your Shelter's Culinary Toolkit

Item	Quantity per Person	Notes
Canned food	20–30 cans	Look for pull-tabs. Can openers are betrayal-prone.
Water	1 gal/day	Including for "spaghetti hydration events"
Fuel	1 small unit/day	Preferably flameless or boring
Toilet bucket	1 per 4 humans	The true throne of the apocalypse
Trash bags	2/day	One for trash, one for shame
Hand sanitizer	1 bottle	Guard it like a relic

Item	Quantity per Person	Notes
Bleach	1 quart	Unscented. Unless you're into lavender death.
Air freshener	Optional	Emotional support only.

"Someday, you'll tell your grandchildren about this.
Or someone will. You'll probably still be in the shelter.

Lesson 11.

Post-Blast Communication Methods

How to Speak to the World When the World Is Mostly Ash

"In the early days of the apocalypse, you'll miss two things: coffee and signal bars."

Just because civilization is taking a nap doesn't mean communication is off the table. This chapter covers real Cold War communication techniques — plus a few low-tech hacks — for reaching out, calling in, or at least yelling *"We're still alive"* into the static void.

1. Let's Check the Obvious: Electronics Are Probably Dead

If the nuke came with an **EMP** (electromagnetic pulse), there's a good chance your electronics are:

- Fried

- Bricked

- Now serving as emotional support bricks

If you were smart (or lucky), and you had a radio in a **Faraday cage** — congrats, you now own the 1960s equivalent of Twitter: static and maybe a guy in Kansas reading headlines.

2. The King of Cold War Comms: The Battery-Powered AM/FM/Shortwave Radio

Your best friend post-blast is an **analog, crankable, battery-powered radio**. Bonus if it supports:

- **NOAA weather band**

- **Shortwave (SW)**

- **HAM frequencies**

  Your goal is to listen, not talk. Most of your energy will go into understanding what's left.

Likely Broadcasts (within first 72 hours):

- Emergency instructions from military/continuity government

- Fallout zone updates

- Evacuation orders or shelter extension notices

- Pre-recorded messages on loop (from facilities you've never heard of)

3. Two-Way Communication (If You Must Talk)

If you're desperate enough to try speaking to the radioactive wasteland, here's how:

CB Radio (Citizens Band)

- Limited range (1–5 miles, terrain-dependent)
- Channel 9 = Emergency
- Channel 19 = General info
- Works best outdoors or with external antenna

HAM Radio

- Long-range (10–500+ miles depending on setup)
- Requires license pre-war (not post-war, oddly enough)
- Frequencies to scan:
    - 3.5–4.0 MHz (80 meter band)
    - 7.0–7.3 MHz (40 meter band)
    - 14.0–14.35 MHz (20 meter band)
- Try calling CQ ("seek you") or listen for nets

    "CQ, CQ… This is Fallout Shelter Tango-Romeo… We have canned goods and unresolved trauma. Please respond."

4. Passive Signaling Methods

If you can't transmit, you can still **signal**. Analog never dies.

Roof Messages

- Use paint, tarps, or rocks to spell **HELP**, **ALIVE**, or **NEED WATER**
- Make letters **at least 8 feet tall** — visible to air surveillance or drones
- Optional: Add an arrow to shelter location

Flagging or Cloth Codes

- **White cloth** = peace
- **Red cloth** = medical emergency
- **Yellow** = radiation danger
- **Black X** = confirmed death (morbid but clear)

Caveat: Don't put out signs you can't uphold. "SAFE ZONE HERE" means you'll be hosting — or raided.

5. The Human Element (Scouts, Runners, and Regret)

Eventually, someone might need to leave the shelter. You'll want to prepare them for **contact protocols**:

- Go solo or in pairs, *never in a large group*
- Carry written ID of shelter location
- If leaving messages:
  - Use chalk, grease pencil, or paint
  - Date and time-stamp
  - Indicate status clearly: ALIVE, INJURED, MOVED, etc.

Tips for runners:

- Assume they won't come back
- Equip with map, radiation dosimeter, food, and face covering
- Have a plan if they return... radioactive

Quick Signal Kit (Pre- or Post-Blast)

Item	Use
Battery-powered radio	Lifeline to the world
Faraday bag or box	EMP protection for radios/electronics

Item	Use
CB / HAM handheld	Short- or long-range comms
Chalk / markers	Signaling on walls, roads, doors
Bright cloth / tarp	Passive roof signals
Notepad + pencil	Messaging between scouts/shelters
Mirror or flashlight	Line-of-sight visual signals
Whistle	Shelter alerts (in case of breach)

A Note on Silence

"In the absence of communication, every sound becomes a threat."

Use caution when broadcasting — especially in the later stages. If society has fractured, radio chatter may attract looters, raiders, or the *unwell*. Listen more than you speak. Keep your shelter's location ambiguous until verified help arrives.

"The world may be silent, but that doesn't mean it's over. Sometimes, the static has something to say."

Lesson 12.

Mental Health in a Fallout Shelter — Don't Go Weird

Because You're Trapped in a Box With Your Thoughts (and Steve)

"Day 54. Steve's been replaced by roaches. They're better at poker anyway."

Welcome to Day Who-Knows-What of the post-nuclear funhouse. You've survived the blast, the fallout, and maybe even a heated argument about whether tuna belongs in the ration rotation.
Now comes the real threat: **your mind.**

This chapter covers how to stay sane(ish), manage stress, and prevent your shelter from turning into a psychological escape room with no escape and increasingly weird vibes.

Shelter Syndrome: What Happens When Humans Become Furniture

Symptoms include:

- Talking to cans like they're coworkers

- Naming the dust bunnies

- Replaying your last pre-blast argument with Karen over and over

- Losing track of time, space, or pants

This is **normal.**
This is also **a warning.**

Stage One: Cabin Fever

"Everyone's breathing too loud and I want to punch the sun."

- Irritability

- Restlessness

- Increased sensitivity to noise, smell, and Steve's chewing

- The overwhelming urge to "just get some air"

Combat With:

- Scheduled alone time (rotate who gets the "corner of peace")

- Noise boundaries (quiet hours, designated whistling zones)

- Exercises: pacing, shadow boxing, interpretive rage dance

- Writing things down instead of yelling

"No one should die over a flashlight being clicked too many times. Yet here we are."

Stage Two: Existential Collapse

"What's the point?"

- Depressive withdrawal
- Refusing food or participation
- Staring at the wall like it owes you answers
- Starting conversations with "Remember before?"

Combat With:

- Assigning meaningful tasks (even dumb ones — "Dust Patrol")
- Creating small daily goals:
    - Boil water
    - Invent a board game
    - Write a haiku about beans
- Sharing stories of *why* survival still matters:
    - Family
    - Revenge
    - The dog you left behind that might still be out there

"Hope doesn't have to be realistic. It just has to delay collapse."

Stage Three: The "Don't Go in the Corner" Phase

"Why is Greg mumbling to the toilet bucket?"

This is **late-stage weirdness**:

- Delusions

- Aggression

- Repetitive compulsions (stacking cans, reorganizing dirt)

- Sudden shifts in mood or personality

- Laughing at nothing (not like the rest of us do — worse)

Combat With:

- Immediate group intervention: calm, kind, **firm**

- Isolation if safety becomes an issue

- Rotate tasks, reintroduce novelty

- Sing. Badly. Together.

- Enforce structure like it's oxygen

"The moment someone starts making eye contact with walls, you need a plan."

The Sanity Toolkit

Tool	Use
Notebook + pen	Venting, planning, drawing your descent into madness
Playing cards or dice	Game creation, gambling, strategic distraction
Daily log	Time tracking, routine reinforcement
Paper calendar	Visual progression = visible survival
"Good Memory" journal	One nice thing per person, per day
Drawing materials	Sometimes you need to sketch a squirrel in a hazmat suit
Music or instruments	Even if it's just tapping the bleach bottle in 4/4 time
Shelter mascot	Sock puppet, empty bottle with eyes, whatever works

"Bet you're wishing the bomb got you at this point."

Lesson 13.

Evacuation vs. Shelter-in-Place

How to Tell If It's Finally Time to Leave — Or Time to Dig Deeper

> *"If you're asking whether it's time to evacuate, it's probably already too late. You need a plan not a hunch."*

At some point, the air inside your shelter will start to feel heavy. Maybe it's the humidity. Maybe it's the smell. Maybe it's the unbearable psychological weight of your third week with Uncle Dave. Either way, the question will come:

"Should we leave?"

This chapter helps you answer that — using government doctrine, empirical decay timelines, and a generous helping of **don't-be-an-idiot logic.**

Shelter-in-Place: The Default Until Proven Otherwise

If you're unsure, **you stay.**
If you *think* it might be okay, **you still stay.**
If you hear voices outside calling your name, **you definitely stay.**

Why Shelter Wins (Statistically and Biologically):

- Fallout decays rapidly in first 72 hours

- Radiation drops to survivable levels after ~2 weeks

- Outside air, surfaces, and water are guaranteed contaminated early on

- Venturing out too soon **kills more people than staying put ever did**

> *"Curiosity didn't kill the cat. The cat opened the door and got 300 Rads to the liver."*

When *Not* to Stay

Shelter-in-place is only safe if your shelter **remains viable.** That means:

Condition	Response
Structural collapse or breach	Leave (to alternate shelter if possible)
Flooding or fire	Leave immediately
Rising internal radiation (from contaminated person/item)	Evacuate or isolate source
Medical emergency that cannot be managed inside	Controlled exit only
Depletion of all food and water before safe exit window	Desperate, but may require planned exfil

Never leave due to:

- Cabin fever

- Boredom

- That one guy who *swears* the air "smells fine now"

Signs It Might Be Time to Leave

Use this checklist **no sooner than Day 14** unless forced:

- ☑ Radiation levels outside below 1 mR/hr

- ☑ Fallout visually absent for 7+ days

- ☑ No new fallout detected on surfaces after controlled test

- ☑ Group members are stable and capable of walking

- ☑ Communication attempts (radio, flags, scouts) return nothing

- ☑ Internal resources are down to <2 days of supply

- ☑ You have a **destination** (not just a feeling)

Preparing for an Exit: The Fallout Field Trip Kit

If you do decide to leave, you are now **navigating an unknown environment under duress**. Dress like it.

The Minimum "Don't Die Outside" Loadout:

Item	Notes
Sturdy boots	No sandals in the wasteland
Mask / respirator	N95 minimum; cloth = decoration
Gloves	Work gloves or nitrile overwraps
Long-sleeve layers	Prevents contact contamination
Hood / hat	Hair catches fallout — cover it

Item	Notes
Trash bags	Body bags, ponchos, ground cover, or dignity
Water + iodine tabs	Assume all external sources are poisoned
Radiation dosimeter	If available — monitor and retreat if rising
Signal markers	Bright tape, chalk, mirror
ID and shelter return card	"We lived here. We mattered."

Don't Just Leave — Leave a Mark

Before you go, make sure to:

- Mark your shelter with status ("EVACUATED — DAY 17")

- Leave a note with time, destination, and survivor count

- Seal any waste or sensitive items

- Mark paths with visible trail signs every 100 meters if possible

You're not just walking away. You're giving someone else a chance to understand what happened here.

Tactical Movement Rules

1. Move at dawn or dusk

2. Stick to hard surfaces if possible (less fallout accumulation)

3. Avoid bodies of water, ditches, and anything that looks suspiciously wet

4. Take breaks in high ground or protected cover

5. Stay calm, quiet, and directional — don't wander

6. Assume *nothing* is safe until tested or proven otherwise

Emotional Reality Check

Leaving the shelter feels like a rescue.

> *"It isn't. It's a second survival attempt — with fewer supplies and more unknowns."*

Don't let false hope get people killed.

Final Go-or-No-Go Questions

- Has the fallout map stabilized?

- Do you have protective gear?

- Is the group physically capable of sustained travel?

- Do you have a confirmed destination or goal?

- Can you leave a record of where you went?

If the answer is "no" to most of these… dig deeper. Wait longer. Ration tighter.

"Leaving the shelter means entering a world you didn't make — and can't trust.
Sometimes, surviving means staying put. Other times, it means moving carefully, with a plan and a prayer."

Section III

Surviving the Weeks That Follow

Lesson 14.

Disease, Dust, and Dead Neighbors

The Real Apocalypse Is a Low-Grade Infection

> *"If the radiation didn't get you, the bacteria are still taking bets."*

The bombs were dramatic. The dust was cinematic. But your actual cause of death in this brave new world will likely be a mix of **bad air, bad hygiene, and someone else's poorly timed cough**.

This chapter focuses on what comes after the mushroom clouds — when the real apocalypse begins: **biohazard edition**.

The Triple Threat: Post-Blast Biological Hazards

1. Infectious Disease

- Poor sanitation + tight quarters = outbreak city
- Common culprits:
    - Diarrhea-causing bacteria (E. coli, Shigella)
    - Respiratory infections (influenza, TB, unknown weirdness)
    - Skin infections from minor wounds

2. Contaminated Dust

- Fallout isn't just radioactive — it's **gross**
- Ash, debris, decomposing matter, dead animals... all aerosolized
- Inhalation causes:
    - Pneumonitis (inflammation of the lungs)
    - Nausea and long-term lung scarring
    - "Why do I taste drywall?" syndrome

3. Unattended Death

- Bodies = rot = flies = disease
- A dead neighbor in a sealed building is **not a neutral event**
- Improper disposal becomes a serious health hazard within days

"There's no morgue anymore. Just gravity, tarp, and discretion."

Disease Prevention: Your Shelter as a Bio-Fortress

Rule	Action
Hands off the face	Sanitize before eating or touching your face
Rotate cleaning duty	Surfaces every 12–24 hours
Isolate the sick	Mask them, separate them, *don't argue about it*
Boil your water	If it wasn't sealed, treat it like a threat
Watch for signs	Diarrhea, rashes, unexplained fever = isolate immediately
Keep small wounds clean	Even papercuts can turn on you now

Shelter Triage: Managing a Sick Person Without Medicine

If someone gets sick, you don't treat them — you manage them.

Isolation Protocol:

- Set up a corner or sealed side room (plastic sheeting + tape works)
- Give separate utensils, bedding, waste bucket
- Assign a single caretaker
- Everyone else: mask up, sanitize often

Symptoms to Take Seriously:

- Persistent diarrhea
- Vomiting after Day 3
- Bleeding gums or skin (late-stage radiation or infection)
- Fever > 101°F for more than 24 hours
- Coughing blood (cool in movies, bad in real life)

The Dead Among You

It happens.

Whether it's a stranger you couldn't save, a neighbor who didn't shelter, or someone inside who didn't make it — **you now have a corpse problem**.

"In a survival scenario, death becomes a logistical event."

Disposal Options (Ranked by Sanity):

1. **Outside Burial** (if safe to exit)

   - Shallow trench (18–36 inches), away from water sources
   - Wrap in plastic or tarp, mark clearly
   - Consider tagging with date + ID if possible

2. **Above-Ground Containment**

   - Wrap body tightly (plastic, tarp, etc.)
   - Double-seal in bags or body sack

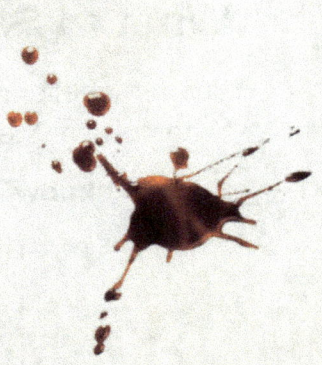

- Move to sealed room or storage chamber
- Label it. Cover it. Let it go.

3. **Last Resort: Room Quarantine**

- Seal off a room completely
- Block vents
- Post a warning
- Understand that psychologically, this is the worst option

Post-Apocalyptic Infection Control Kit

Item	Use
Bleach (5%)	Surface sanitizing, water treatment
Hand sanitizer	Routine hygiene
Face masks	For sick persons and caregivers
Plastic sheeting + duct tape	Quarantine zone setup
Nitrile gloves	Wound care, corpse handling
Thermometer	Track sickness progression
Oral rehydration salts	Diarrhea management
Garbage bags	Multi-use for disposal and isolation
Lemon or vinegar	Disinfectant alternative
Bucket with lid	Isolation waste management

What to Say to the Living When Death Happens

You are sheltering with people you care about. Or tolerate. Or owe your life to. When one of them dies, **you must do two things**:

1. **Acknowledge it**.

- "They didn't make it."
- "They were part of this place."
- "They mattered." Say it. Out loud.

2. **Then act.**

   - Make a plan.

   - Don't delay.

   - Show others that you can handle what the world throws at you — even this.

"Death isn't the end in a shelter. It's a contamination vector."

Daily Shelter Bio-Security Routine

- Wipe down high-touch surfaces (handles, containers, sleeping area)

- Wash hands before food prep and after latrine

- Sanitize water collection gear

- Log any new symptoms

- Rotate bedding or wipe with disinfectant

- Burn trash if it's safe. Otherwise, seal and isolate.

"Disease is patient. It doesn't knock like the bomb did. It waits for you to get tired, lazy, or sad — and then it enters."

Stay clean. Stay alert. Stay a little paranoid.

Lesson 15.

Water Procurement and Purification (Long-Term)

Because You Can't Just Drink Hope

> *"Humans can survive three weeks without food. Three days without water. And about three seconds after trusting a 'natural spring' post-nuke."*

Water is no longer just a luxury or an eco-discussion point — it's now your most precious resource. The water you drink is either going to **sustain you**, **slowly poison you**, or **guarantee a very intimate few hours with your shelter's waste bucket**.

In this chapter, we leave behind bottled reserves and move into long-term strategies: **finding**, **testing**, and **purifying** water in a world where most sources are radioactive, contaminated, or both.

Stage 1: Use What You've Got (Before It Goes Bad)

Before you go scavenging puddles or licking condensation off tarp walls, make sure you've fully exhausted your **initial reserves**.

Safe Initial Sources:

- Sealed bottled water

- Water heater tank (30–50 gallons)

- Toilet tank (not the bowl, you animal)

- Canned goods (fruit syrup, soup liquid)

- Radiator water (only if pre-blast and non-toxic)

> *"Don't laugh — that half-can of can of peaches is now hydration and dessert."*

Stage 2: Scouting for New Sources

Once the sealed stash runs dry, you'll need to become a **hydrated detective**.

Source	Viability	Notes
Rainwater	✅	Best source after 2+ weeks. Filter + boil.
Rooftop runoff	⚠	Avoid if roof is covered in fallout dust
Deep well water	✅	Protected if sealed, test if possible
Rivers/streams	⚠	Must filter and boil. Avoid near urban zones
Lakes/ponds	⚠	High contamination risk — last resort
Snow/ice	⚠	Must melt and purify. Snow ≠ sterile
Puddles/ drainage	❌	Don't. Just... don't.

<u>IMPORTANT</u>- THE FOLLOWING INFORMATION COULD SAVE YOUR LIFE

"If it smells like death or looks like soup, it's not water — it's just something else that wants to kill you."

Stage 3: Purification Methods (aka 'Not Dying From a Sip')

Once you *think* the water might be viable, it still isn't. Not yet. Now we clean it.

Boiling (Best All-Purpose Method)

- Bring water to a **rolling boil for 10+ minutes**
- Kills bacteria, viruses, and parasites

- Doesn't remove chemicals, heavy metals, or radiation
- Requires fuel — budget carefully

Chemical Treatment

- **Bleach**: 2 drops per quart (clear, unscented 5–6% household bleach)
  - Wait 30 min
  - Water should have faint chlorine smell
- **Iodine tabs**: Works, but tastes like regret and thyroids
- **Water purification tablets**: Stockpile these before the world ends

Filtration (Pre-Treatment)

Use to remove **debris, cloudiness, and floating horrors**

- Cloth filter (bandana, T-shirt)
- Sand + charcoal + gravel gravity filter (DIY stacked bottle method)
- Commercial ceramic or carbon filter (if you're lucky)

"If the water looks like iced tea but came from a ditch, trust your gut. And then purify so and your gut don't end up back in the ditch."

Dealing with Radiation in Water

Here's the bad news: **you can't boil radiation out**.
Here's the worse news: **you probably don't have lab-grade filters**.

Best Practices:

- Wait at least 7–14 days after fallout to collect surface water
- Let sediment settle before filtering
- Use **ion exchange resins** or special clay/sand filters (if available)
- Collect **rainwater** from freshly wiped surfaces only
- **Never drink water exposed to visible fallout dust**

"Radiation doesn't care if you're thirsty. Your kidneys, however, do."

Long-Term Water Toolkit

Item	Purpose
Stocked bleach (unscented)	Chemical disinfection
Large pot or kettle	Boiling
Fire source or heat plate	Sustained boiling
Charcoal/sand filter materials	Physical filtration
Plastic sheeting & buckets	Rainwater collection
Water containers (food-safe)	Clean storage
Iodine or chlorine tabs	Portable purification
Coffee filters or cloth	Sediment pre-filter
DIY gravity filter bottle	Makeshift setup
Labeling tape	Mark purified vs. unfiltered

Warning Signs of Bad Water

Even after treatment, water can still go rogue. Look out for:

- Persistent cloudiness

- Bad smell (sulfur, decay, fuel)

- Oily surface sheen

- Floating "stuff" that resists filtration

- Metallic taste

- Immediate nausea after drinking (you blew it)

"Remember: Dehydration is awful. But it's better than diarrhea during a lockdown."

Daily Water Strategy

- Ration 0.5–1 gallon per person per day

- Boil daily batches (if fuel allows)

- Use separate containers for:
  - Raw collection
  - Treated water
  - Emergency only backup
- Rotate your stock if you're collecting rainwater
- Write purification date on containers (use tape, marker, ash, whatever)

"In the post-nuclear world, clean water is a religion.
Worship carefully, and don't drink the false gods."

Lesson 16.

Barter Economy 101: Beans, Booze, and Bullets

Because Paper Money Burns Better Than It Spends

"Welcome to the end of the global supply chain. Hope you've got something someone wants."

The financial system you once knew — debit cards, money transfers, overpriced coffee apps — has been obliterated. In its place rises the **barter economy**, where **usefulness, scarcity, and trust** are the new currency. This chapter teaches you how to trade, haggle, and not get killed doing it.

Why Barter Works When Banks Don't

No electricity = no banks
No communication = no coordination
No police = no real consequences

What remains is the **oldest economic model on Earth**:

> "I have something. You need it. What will you give me?"

If you're lucky, it's a straightforward trade.
If you're unlucky, it's a negotiation with a guy named Crow who smells like meth and carries a crossbow made from plumbing parts.

The Three Pillars of Barter Value

1. **Utility** – Can it save someone's life or make it less miserable?

2. **Portability** – Is it small and easy to carry without dying for it?

3. **Preservability** – Does it last? Or rot? Or explode when dropped?

Top 10 Post-Collapse Barter Items

Item	Why It's Valuable
Clean Water	It's life. Period.
Food (esp. canned)	Lightweight, high-cal, low prep
Booze	Disinfectant, morale, currency, bad decision fuel
Ammo (.22, 9mm, shotgun shells)	Small, useful, lethal, tradable
Painkillers / Antibiotics	Worth more than gold
Cigarettes / Coffee / Nicotine gum	Addicts have needs — and offers
Lighters / Matches / Fire starters	Heat, cooking, signaling
Batteries	Especially AA, AAA, CR123 — the apocalypse runs on flashlights

Item	Why It's Valuable
Soap / Hygiene items	No one wants to trade with the smelly guy
Condoms	Disease control, stress relief, and surprisingly good for water sealing

"Barter is not charity. It's desperation with manners."

What NOT to Trade (If You Like Breathing)

- **Weapons**: Don't arm someone you don't trust

- **Shelter location info**: Your coordinates are not for sale

- **All your meds or ammo**: Keep a fallback

- **Luxury items too early**: No one wants jewelry during gastrointestinal collapse

- **Knowledge of your stockpile**: Oversharing = future home invasion

"The first rule of barter club: You have less than you say, and more than you look."

Barter Etiquette (aka How Not to Get Stabbed)

Rule	Survival Benefit
Meet in neutral zones	Never bring strangers to base
Bring a backup	Quiet muscle keeps things civil
Show but don't flash	Reveal one trade item at a time
Don't insult offers	A bad deal is better than a bad wound
Pre-arrange signals	One blink = too risky. Two = go loud.
Use small denominations	Break big items into tradable units (e.g., water in 16oz bottles)

"You're not negotiating a car loan — you're avoiding your next funeral."

Shelter-Based Trade Strategy

You don't always need to go out into barterland. You can become **a node in the network** — a known spot for quiet, clean, fair trade.

To do this:

- Create a **barter ledger**: What came in, what went out
- Maintain **neutral reputation**: "They're fair. Don't mess with them."
- Offer trade days — fixed times, controlled guests
- Never reveal **full inventory** to traders
- Be known for **one item** (water, ammo, medical, info)

  "If people think you're useful but replaceable, you're safe. If they think you're essential, you're a target."

Example Trade Values (Very Rough)

Item	Typical Trade Value
1 can of beans	2 water bottles or 1 AA battery
1 bottle of bleach	3–5 water purification tabs
10 rounds of .22LR	1 first aid kit or 1 MRE
1 bottle of whiskey	1 full day's ration + minor meds
1 painkiller tablet	Anything someone will part with
1 condom	1 can of food (especially late-stage)

All values fluctuate wildly. As do tempers. Use discretion.

Final Notes on Trust

Barter doesn't require friendship — but it does require rules.

- **Repeat traders** = reputation = stability

- **Loose lips** = raiders = bad endings

- **One-time exchanges** = short memory, less risk

"Trust is a currency too. Just don't spend it all in one place."

Lesson 17.

Signal Fires, Symbols, and Rescue Possibilities

Because Maybe Someone's Still Out There

> *"Survival isn't just about hiding. Eventually, it's about being seen — by the right people."*

You've made it through the blast, the fallout, the long haul, the food roulette, the bucket politics, and the weirdness. You've rationed, coped, and possibly choreographed a shelter musical to maintain morale.

Now comes the question: **Can you be found? Should you even try?**

This chapter covers the subtle art of **being noticed without getting looted**, and the fading-but-not-yet-extinct hope of **rescue.**

Should You Try to Signal?

Short answer: **Not during the danger window** (first 72–168 hours post-blast). Longer answer: **Only when:**

- Fallout risk has dropped
- You're stable enough to receive contact
- You're not attracting the wrong kind of attention
- You have a plan if signaling works (or doesn't)

> *"Shouting into the void is therapeutic. But sometimes, it shouts back."*

Signal Fires: Primitive, Reliable, Risky

Pros	Cons
Visible from distance or air	Uses fuel you may need
Easy to construct	May expose your location
Works day and night	Requires maintenance

How to Build a Survival Signal Fire:

- Use **triangular or cross pattern** (3 fires = distress)
- Burn near **high ground or open field**
- Add **green plant matter or rubber** to create smoke
- Build with layers: dry wood base, damp smoky topping
- Prepare **but don't light** until conditions are safe

Nighttime bonus: Flashing lights or strobe (if you've got them) = excellent attention grabber.

Ground Symbols & Roof Markings

Think **old-school**: visible shapes, bold letters, contrasting color

Symbol	Meaning
"HELP" / "SOS"	Basic distress
Large X	Occupied / supplies needed
Arrow →	Direction of movement
Circle with dot (☉)	Shelter present
"WATER" / "FOOD"	Specific needs
Your shelter's symbol	Custom, repeatable ID for future contact

Rules for Visibility:

- Minimum 8-foot lettering
- Use rocks, logs, white sheets, anything bold
- Place where aerial or drone visibility is possible
- Maintain, refresh, or remove symbols as needed

"Just don't draw a giant happy face. That's how cults start."

Radio Signaling (If You're Lucky)

If you've preserved a radio setup, now's the time to **talk back**.

Best Practices:

- Announce shelter ID + status on a repeating schedule (e.g. top of each hour)

- Use standard emergency frequencies:

  - CB: Channel 9

  - HAM: 3.5–4.0 MHz, 7.0–7.3 MHz, 14.0–14.35 MHz

  - Marine: Channel 16 (156.8 MHz)

- Use simple language:

  > "Fallout Shelter Alpha. 3 survivors. Day 20. Request contact or assistance. Broadcasting hourly."

  "Repeat. Don't ramble. You're not doing a podcast."

Passive Signal Options

If you can't broadcast live, **leave signs for others**:

- **Mirror or metal flashes** during daytime

- **Painted symbols on trees, rocks, or roads**

- **Hanging fabric** (white = peaceful, red = medical, yellow = radiation, black = death site)

- **Directional trails** using chalk, ribbons, or rocks

- **Paper messages in sealed bags** under rock markers

Responding to Outside Signals (Tread Carefully)

If you **receive** a signal or contact:

Signal	Interpretation
Voice over radio	Human. Verify identity. Use code phrases if planned.
Flashing light in pattern	Human. Pattern = intelligence. Respond with same.
Loudspeaker / sirens	Government or organized group. Stay hidden and observe before engaging.

Signal	Interpretation
Vehicles with markings	Military/civil rescue possible. Wait, watch, then signal with caution.
Individual yelling randomly	Possibly desperate. Possibly dangerous.

General Rule:
Approach slowly. With cover. Assume uncertainty. **Plan for extraction if it goes south.**

> *"Not everyone who survived is stable. And not everyone who's stable is friendly."*

Quick Rescue-Ready Prep

- Create signal fire structure in advance

- Paint or prep rooftop message

- Designate a radio operator and routine

- Prepare basic shelter info card (survivor count, medical needs)

- Pre-write distress message in waterproof envelope

- Discuss contact plan with group (who speaks, who watches, who flanks)

> *"Being found isn't the end. It's a new beginning — with strangers, probably wearing body armor."*

Make it count. Make it safe. And maybe, just maybe, make it home.

Section IV: Appendices & Extras

Because information still matters

Appendix A: Fallout Decay Curves and Exposure Tables

7/10 Rule Reference:

- After 7× more time, radiation = 1/10th the previous level

Time Since Blast	Approx. % of Original Radiation	Notes
1 hour	100%	Death soup
7 hours	~10%	Still dangerous
49 hours	~1%	Safer with protection
2 weeks	~0.1%	Consider outside movement

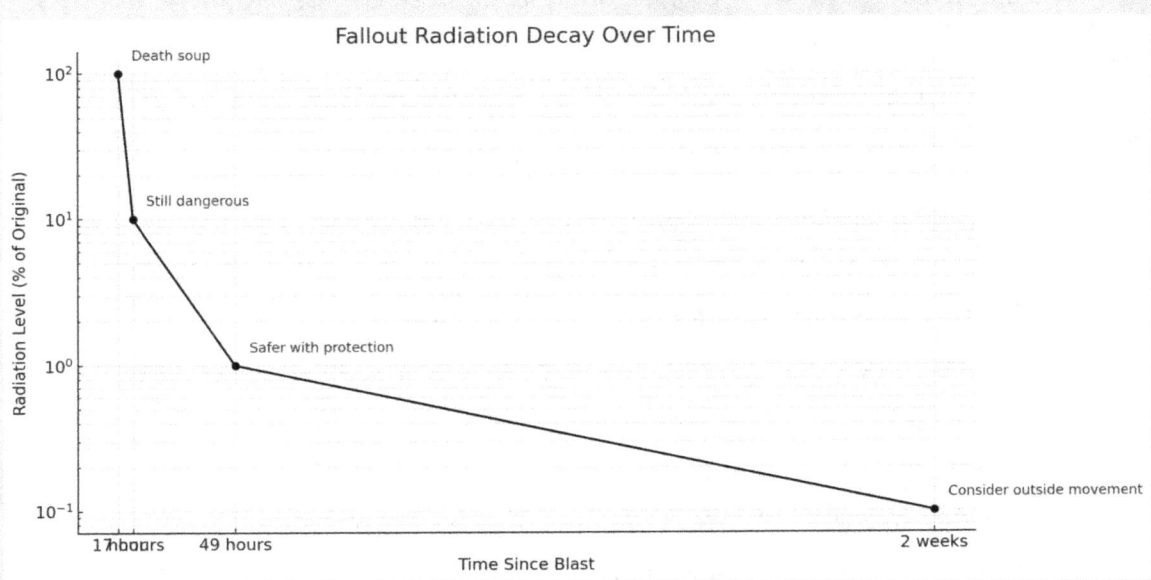

Appendix B: Printable Shelter Quick Reference Sheet

"If you're reading this, things have gone sideways. Hopefully you printed it in advance."

72-Hour Survival Checklist (Assumes fallout is actively falling or imminent)

Immediate Priorities

1. **Get underground or under mass**
2. **Avoid external exposure for at least 72 hours**
3. **Begin ration tracking**
4. **Seal the shelter — air, light, and guilt stay outside**

Stay calm. Irrational decisions are harder to undo after irradiation.

✅ **Shelter**
- ☐ Get underground, behind concrete, or under at least 6 inches of dense material (dirt, books, bricks, water tanks)
- ☐ Seal cracks/vents with plastic bags, tape, towels
- ☐ Stay inside for **minimum 72 hours**

✅ **Radiation Barrier Enhancements**
- ☐ Stack mass *between* you and outside (not above you if unstable)
- ☐ Use water jugs, furniture, dirt bags, books
- ☐ Shelter-in-shelter: a makeshift cocoon (e.g., under a table with dense shielding)

✅ **Air Management**
- ☐ Block external airflow unless you have a filtered intake
- ☐ Avoid using fire or open flame — consumes oxygen, adds CO
- ☐ Breathe slow. Talk less. Smell nothing.

☑ **Water**
- ☐ Minimum: 1 gallon/person/day
- ☐ Prioritize sealed water; do **not** collect rain within first 2 weeks
- ☐ Purify only **after** 2 weeks or if from sealed sources

☑ **Food**
- ☐ Eat perishables first
- ☐ High-calorie, low-prep foods: peanut butter, protein bars, jerky, etc.
- ☐ Ration: Small frequent meals to manage energy and morale

☑ **Sanitation**
- ☐ Bucket toilet + trash bags + kitty litter/sawdust
- ☐ Wet wipes or vinegar water for sponge baths
- ☐ Keep waste sealed and stored away from living area

☑ **Medical**
- ☐ Basic first aid: cuts, burns, fever, dehydration
- ☐ Use potassium iodide (KI) only if advised and within timeframe
- ☐ Watch for signs of radiation sickness (nausea, weakness, confusion)

☑ **Communication**
- ☐ AM/FM radio with batteries or hand crank
- ☐ Keep phone off to save battery; check signal intermittently
- ☐ Assume no help is coming for 72–96 hours

☑ **Morale**
- ☐ Rotate tasks, keep a journal, avoid panic
- ☐ Share food and warmth
- ☐ Don't stare at the door

Appendix C: Potassium Iodide (KI) – The Thyroid's Wingman

What It Does:

Potassium iodide (KI) is not an anti-radiation pill. Let's repeat that louder for the bunker crowd:

> **KI does *not* protect against all radiation.**

What it *does* do is saturate your thyroid gland with stable (non-radioactive) iodine so that when radioactive iodine-131 starts flying around after a nuclear detonation or reactor meltdown, your thyroid **shrugs and ignores it**.

This helps prevent **thyroid cancer** — particularly in children, young adults, and people who don't already glow in the dark.

KI is **only helpful for radioactive iodine exposure**, which is common in **reactor accidents** and **some nukes** — but not all nuclear detonations. So keep it in your kit, but **<u>don't rely on it like it's a hazmat force field</u>**.

How and When to Take It:

- **Timing is everything.** KI works best if taken *shortly before* or *within hours* after exposure to radioactive iodine.

- Take **once daily for a few days**, depending on public health guidance.

- Do **not** take it preemptively "just in case." That's how you get sick from the pill instead of the fallout.

Age Group	Typical Dosage
Adults (>18 yrs)	130 mg
Children (3–18)	65 mg
Infants (<3 yrs)	16–32 mg

Only take for 7–10 days post-exposure. Always follow local health guidance during a nuclear event. Preferably from someone who didn't get their license in a cereal box.

Where to Get It:

- **Over-the-counter** in most U.S. states (Amazon, Ready.gov recommendations, or pharmacies)

- Brands like *IOSAT*, *ThyroSafe*, or *ThyroShield*

- Government may distribute it in emergencies if supply chains still exist

Shelf Life & Storage:

- **Shelf life**: Typically 5–7 years if stored sealed in a cool, dry, dark place

- Tablets past expiration **may still retain partial potency** — but efficacy is not guaranteed

- Do **not** expose to moisture — it degrades faster than society

Warnings & Side Effects:

- Common: Upset stomach, allergic reaction, weird metallic taste

- Rare but serious: Overactive thyroid, rash, salivary gland swelling

- Avoid if allergic to iodine, shellfish, or sarcastic medical advice

Appendix D: Fallout Zone Map

"In Case You'd Like to Know Which Direction Not to Run."

Remember fallout is the radioactive dust and debris kicked up by a nuclear detonation. The lower winds carry heavier particles downwind over the first 20–100 miles. Lighter particles rise higher and ride upper-atmosphere winds — including jet streams — sometimes traveling hundreds or thousands of miles before settling.

1. Sample CONUS Fallout Plume Overlays

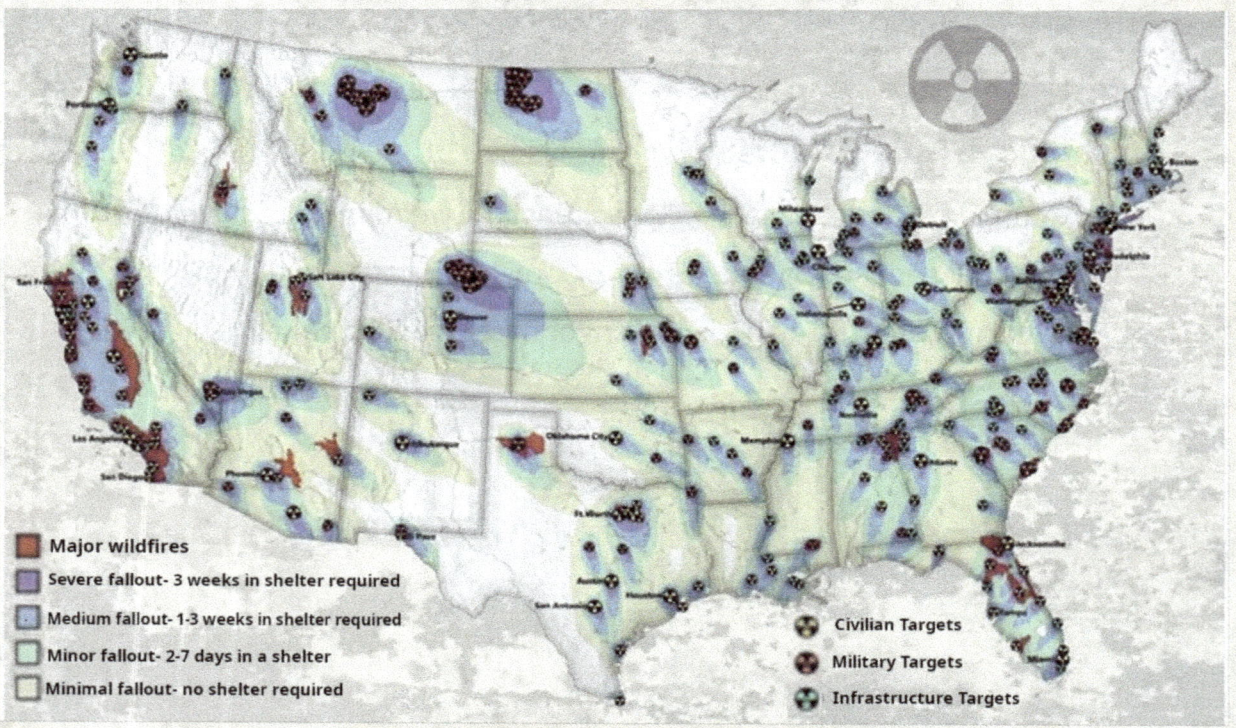

Fallout dispersal dependent on local winds and actual targets

Appendix E: Kearny Fallout Meter (KFM)

"You didn't think I'd leave you hanging"

Developed by Cresson Kearny at Oak Ridge National Laboratory, the Kearny Fallout Meter (KFM) is a civil defense instrument that can be built in a few hours from readily available materials: a soup can, aluminum foil, thread, plastic, wire, bits of drywall, and tape. The only tools required are a pair of scissors, a hammer and a nail. Despite its simplicity, it is said to be able to measure exposure rates from 30 mR/hr to 43 R/hr with an accuracy of plus or minus 25%.

The KFM is actually an aluminum foil electroscope, the body of which is made from a soup can (ca. 2 5/8" in diameter and 4" high). Some type of desiccant (e.g., heated gypsum from drywall) is stored in the bottom. In this particular design, the desiccant is covered with a perforated metal disk (the top of the can with holes punched it). A paper scale, ca. 10 mm x 50 mm, is glued to the perforated disk so that it can be viewed by looking down through the top of the can. In later versions of the KFM, the scale is attached to the clear plastic sheet stretched across the top of the can, and the perforated metal disk covering the desiccant is done away with. Two aluminum leaves (1.5" x 1 L") are suspended above the scale from parallel nylon threads attached to the top of the can. The leaves, made from eight-ply aluminum foil, are charged via a 3" insulated "charging wire," bare at each end, that penetrates the plastic sheet. The charge itself is created by rapidly unwinding a piece of scotch tape.

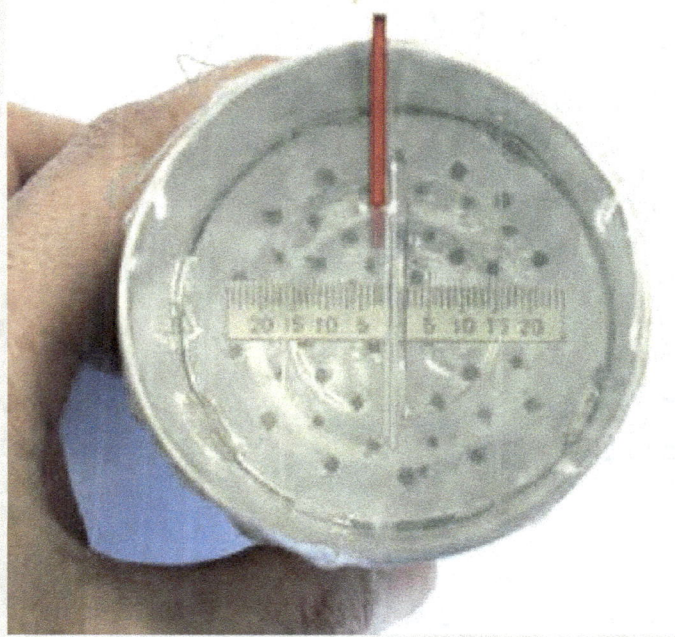

After being charged, the leaves separate and the spacing (in mm) of the bottom edges of the leaves on the scale is noted. After the exposure (15 seconds to 1 hour), when the leaves have moved closer together, the spacing of the leaf edges is noted once more. The decrease in the spacing is converted to the exposure by referring to the calibration table taped to the side of the can.

The calibration table, as well as templates and instructions for the meter's construction, can be found in "The KFM, A Homemade Yet Accurate and Dependable Fallout Meter."

Kearny's KFM can be considered an improved version of a home-made electroscope described by Callahan and Kaplan in 1960. Kearny identified the following advantages of his KFM over Callahan and Kaplan's electroscope:

- Its maximum measurable exposure (full discharge) was 200 mR vs 5 mR.
- It could operate under humid conditions.
- It was easier to construct.

Donated by the Federal Emergency Management Agency courtesy of Carl Siebentritt.

Appendix F: Water Safety Quick Guide

Contamination Warning Signs:

- Cloudy water

- Metallic or chemical smell

- Oil-like surface sheen

- Immediate nausea post-drink

Purification Methods:

- Boil 10+ mins (does not remove radiation)

- Bleach: 2 drops/qt, wait 30 mins

- Use carbon/charcoal filter (if available)

- Combine sediment filtration + chemical disinfection

Do Not Drink:

- Water exposed to fallout dust

- Puddles or runoff within 7 days of blast

- Water from open containers outside shelter

Safe Sources (Post 2 Weeks):

- Rain from cleaned surfaces

- Deep well water (sealed)

- Snow/ice (melted and treated)

When in doubt — treat, wait, and never assume it's safe without purification.

Appendix G: Source Notes and Document Index

Includes:

- "Family Shelter Designs" (1967, U.S. Office of Civil Defense)

- "Radiological Defense: Planning and Operations Guide" (FEMA, 1972)

- "Kearny Fallout Meter" Manual (Oak Ridge National Lab)

- Civil Defense Museum Archives (civildefensemuseum.com)

- National Emergency Training Center Document Library

Appendix H: About This Guide

Compiled, reformatted, and expanded from public domain Cold War documents and modern survival best practices.

Prepared in collaboration with AI and human co-authorship for readability, humor, and maximum practical use under duress.

Not affiliated with any agency. Use at your own risk. Good luck.

www.ingramcontent.com/pod-product-compliance
Lightning Source LLC
Chambersburg PA
CBHW082227140626
46556CB00020B/3380